ABOUT THIS BOOK

OneAccord is a company comprised of people passionate about building value. Often, value creation comes through increasing top line revenue growth. For this reason, OneAccord Partners created this compilation of chapters about attracting more customers and growing revenue. Whether you're a salesperson just getting your start or an owner with 40 years' experience, this book is a resource to help you increase your revenue and build lasting value.

COPYRIGHT

VALUES THAT SELL

INTRODUCTION BY #1 BESTSELLING AUTHOR
JUSTIN BLANEY AND
CONTRIBUTIONS BY **JEFF ROGERS**
GLENN HANSEN RICHARD BRUNE
DEAN KATO JOHN KAMINSKI
A ONEACCORD RESOURCE

TABLE OF CONTENTS

INTRODUCTION

By Justin Blaney

In the great movie commentary on sales, *Tommy Boy*, we learn every salesperson needs to find their own style. I believe everyone can be great at sales. It doesn't matter if you're an introvert or extrovert, short or tall, nasal or deep voiced, charismatic or dull, a genius or average, you can be great at sales. The characteristics that make you unique, the parts of you that you can't change, are far less important to your success as a salesperson than the factors under your control. Depending on our picture of what a salesperson is, and what level of baggage we bring, it's understandable to think "I can't be good at sales" or "I don't want to be thought of as a salesperson." But these thoughts are based on incorrect notions; either being great at sales requires certain traits we cannot change in ourselves, or being great at sales means letting go of our values. I've met incredible salespeople of every shape, color and personality. Some of them have written chapters in this book and are the last people to play the role of a slick salesperson who is only interested in getting into your pocketbook.

The worst thing any sales person can do is try to be someone they are not or sell their values for a short-term increase in profits. So, like Tommy, to become better at sales you might first have to let go of some of what you've seen in other successful sales people and accept that what works for others may not work for you.

You might be a business owner or CEO with a lifetime of experience, or you might just be getting your start in sales. The truth is, we are all sales people and we all have learned how to influence others. However, many of us pick up a few bad habits along the way that technically work, but hurt us in the long run. So no matter who you are, or your background, if you are interested in growing your business, exceeding your quota, or increasing revenue for your organization, this book is for you. And even if the values are familiar, I find a reminder helpful in the continual process of ridding ourselves of those bad habits we pick up from time to time.

These are thoughts anyone can adopt to become more successful. They don't require you to have charisma, good looks or the ability to tell great stories at a dinner table. They may, on the other hand, require patience, a giving philosophy, humility, and the ability to put other people, whether customers or employees, ahead of your own immediate interests. The good news is, anyone can adopt these ideas. All it takes is willingness and time. And, like Tommy, finding the style that fits who we really are.

VALUE 1: KNOW WHY

By John Kaminski

Let's assume you want to be successful. You figure out what you want to do, set goals and make plans to achieve them. Do you know why you want what you want? I mean really know why?

Statistics show that at best only 30% of objectives are achieved. Unless you are in the business of baseball, 30% is not very good. One contributing factor to this low rate of success happens right at the beginning. Typically, we decide what we want to do, then immediately jump to figuring out how to do it. If you don't know why you want what you want, chances are that your goal needs refinement and the likelihood of achieving your vision is not very high.

Here's an example from a conversation I had with a colleague recently. He said he had a goal to earn $200,000 a year. I asked him why.

"Because I have a family to support and that's how much it takes," he replied. I asked him why.

"Well, there's a mortgage, food, clothing, we have a boat…"

"Why is that important," I asked?

"When I was growing up, we had a boat and the times on the boat were some of my greatest memories from my childhood. I want to be able to have that with my kids."

"Ahhh…," I said, "So what you really want is to provide your kids with the same kinds of family bonding experiences you had growing up. That's a bit different than earning $200,000 per year. Are there other ways you might achieve that goal?"

The income is HOW he thought he could achieve what he really wanted. If you jump to the HOW before figuring out WHY, you just might find yourself focused on the wrong things. All of a sudden, you realize your family relationships are suffering because you are working long hours to earn enough to spend time bonding with your family.

The same principles hold true in business. Strategic initiatives are executed to improve the company. Too often, those setting the vision announce the new goals, or the WHAT, then tell HOW the company will accomplish the goals, but never share the WHY.

Say you have a goal to increase sales 20%. On the surface, the reason WHY could be to increase profitability. But why 20%? Why is that the right number? Do costs drop dramatically if you make and sell a certain quantity? Does 20% growth take market share from competition? Is that simply all the growth you believe is realistic?

Let's say you selected 20% because that would maximize your production capacity. If you share that WHY with your employees, maybe someone identifies a way to produce more. Sharing WHY helps to align your team with your objective and provides insight into the foundational values that drive the goal, which affect the decisions we need to make when working towards the goal.

When you think you know what you want, take the time to figure out why you want it. And to really figure out why; you usually need to go many levels deep. When you share your vision, make sure you share the WHY.

VALUE 2: ATTRACT GREAT TALENT

By Jeff Rogers

Recently, we talked about factors to consider when properly assessing sales talent and the numerous benefits they bring to your sales organization. This article will focus on what you need to do to attract the right sales talent.

As we all know, great salespeople are compensated extremely well and when this is the case, it can entail considerable expenditure as a percentage of revenue to any corporate entity. In addition, there are significant risks involved when a large pay disbursement is made and a corresponding ROI financial result needs to be produced.

We have heard of companies that "solve" this problem by simply reducing the compensation. The reasoning behind this logic that is most often voiced is that if things don't work out then the company is not out a lot of money.

If you are thinking this is an example of sound logical business thinking, we would ask you to reconsider the notion.

There are many reasons why outstanding sales professionals join companies. Examples would include having great benefits, an outstanding work environment or having a passionate cause. But in this article — we're only focusing on compensation. A truism of sales is that effective salespeople always know how to work their compensation plan to its maximum benefit, which is a critical reason as to why your sales compensation plan must closely align with the business needs of your organization.

Another general truism of effective salespeople is that as part of knowing how to work a compensation plan, the process generally starts with what company they decide to join in the first place. Top sales professionals will generally pick the companies that best know how to properly reward them for their quality work. Competition for sales positions in the types of sales organizations with great compensation and benefits will always be tight.

LET'S CONTRAST THE TWO APPROACHES TO SALES ORGANIZATIONS

- Hire hungry youngsters with a reasonable base of $30k and a chance to make more
- Hire "high-end hunters" – bring in your W2, if it's less than $150k don't apply

First, we will follow the example of the company that offers something akin to $30K base salary with total compensation budgeted to $45-$50K competing for sales staff with the companies that understand the value of a fully dynamic compensation plan. Companies that follow a lower tier compensation model often have sales staff that come and go (high attrition), while at the same time, they have an executive team that readily admits that finding good salespeople is strictly a "hit or miss" proposition. This holds true even if the company is reasonably well-versed at understanding which sales hiring profiles are most appropriate for their company. Paying lower compensation soon becomes its own self-fulfilling prophecy, i.e. "We don't want to spend more money on hiring the new sales representative because hiring for the position usually winds up being a 'hit or miss' endeavor."

SOUND FAMILIAR? THUS BEGINS A NEVER ENDING HIRING AND ATTRITION CIRCLE.

When attrition in a sales organization is high, it can cause innumerable issues. Let's look at the argument from a narrow perspective: Would you rather spend $100K+ in compensation and have a satisfied, high-performing sales representative who is with your company for 10-15 years and generates revenue that more than pays for the company's expenditure? Or, would you rather cycle through paying $45K-$50K annually for sales reps that might stay with you for 18-24 months and are often focused on meaningless sales activity that generates minimal sales production?

Occasionally, you will find first-round talent in the third round. It worked for our intrepid Seattle Seahawks when they drafted Russell Wilson with the 75th overall pick in the 2012 NFL Draft. But 9 times out of 10 you are going to get a third-round talent with a third round draft (i.e. compensation) pick.

We are not telling you to spend haphazardly or carelessly in the attempt to garner great sales talent. There should always be a good process in place whenever you make an important hiring decision. Sales compensation modeling is intricate and there are a number of factors that have to align completely for it to be effective for the company. But when designed properly, an effective sales compensation plan can be constructed to allow you the capability to build a successful, highly talented, low-attrition, outperforming sales team whose members bring highly impactful financial production to your company.

Certainly, even the best sales compensation plan without a corresponding ability to know how to hire correctly can be a recipe for disaster. Our Frontline Perspective: a highly rewarding compensation plan that rewards top talent well while serving the interests of the business can lead to greatly increased revenue and GP. Top sales talent will be attracted enough to start a conversation with your company. With a scarcity of high performing sales talent, compensation is a topic that can give you a needed edge when competing for the best sales staff.

Before you can make this model work, however, you really need to be crisp on your cost of customer acquisition and lifetime value of your customer.

VALUE 3: HIRE WELL

By Jeff Rogers

It is a familiar refrain. The ability to hire great people allows you, as a company, to go out and have outstanding execution as a sales organization. The reason for that is simple. It is people who animate your sales process and give it meaning. The vitality of having a dynamic sales team to implement results within your sales operations cannot be underestimated. While an effective, disciplined sales process is commonly underestimated as a function of driving increased revenue, most companies do, in fact, place an emphasis on trying to hire the best talent they can.

But are they as successful as they could be? And why do some organizations perform consistently well in the sales arena while others muddle through or are constantly having to change their core selling programs in a continual quest to improve a lagging result?

Our view is that it starts with correctly defining and identifying what a successful sales hire is. It is a fairly common observation that many companies focus on quantifiable measures such as "attainment to quota" and "sales rank" to determine who should get into the door to interview. Personality fit to the existing sales culture is usually then determined along with an exploration of previous sales accomplishment in the interview process.

This results in making a final hiring decision that has a varied degree of substance to it. It is a sound general strategy but lacks a level of completeness.

Sales is often the primary revenue producing function of an organization. It proverbially pays the bills and keeps the lights on. And the revenue and profit generated from the sales function essentially pays for everyone's salaries, wages and benefits.

It is important for sales people to produce solid individual numbers. But your top performing sales person, strictly by the numbers, is not necessarily your best salesperson. As a corporate entity or private business, your goal is to continually replicate hiring your best salespeople.

With that said, any number of factors can skew the quantification of sales rank and other numerical performance measures... from misaligned territory opportunity to inappropriate use of system discounting to differing levels of activity in calling on customers. As an example: George quickly burns through 100 leads and becomes the top sales person for the quarter while Jane, your second place salesperson, just misses the top mark. But Jane has taken the time to cultivate great future relationships and places a high emphasis on really understanding her customer's needs. She has accomplished her quarterly result with only 33 direct leads. So which salesperson is better driving your long-term sales success?

THAT IS WHY THE FOLLOWING EQUATION SHOULD DRIVE YOUR HIRING PRACTICES

Sales Behavior + Sales Attitude + Customer & Product Aptitude minus factors of variation in your Sales Process = Performance Result

A common mistake many frontline sales managers make both in managing their team and in conducting hiring decisions is the over reliance on simply managing or hiring to a number. It does seem "safe", doesn't it? It's certainly easy. But "safe" and "easy" can often be very misleading.

When managing and hiring to this new equation, the hiring process itself does become more difficult. But it also yields rich depth in providing clarity to understanding how your sales reps drive revenue creation. And managing to the precepts of the formula delivers a more bountiful revenue result overall. Let's look at the various components of the equation just a little bit more in-depth.

SALES BEHAVIORS

Sales behaviors can be explored through using roleplaying exercises in the interview process. Sales behaviors are important because they translate what actually is happening in the interaction between your salesperson and your customer. Additionally, the study of sales behaviors allows insight into how well sales staff can actually follow specific sales processes.

People who exhibit competent sales behaviors are more readily able to follow a defined sales process. Which brings us to...

SALES ATTITUDE

Attitude is more than just how friendly, positive and upbeat someone is. The larger driving point of assessing this personal trait is to understand how malleable someone will be to receiving coaching, development and training and how willing they will be to conform to the standards outlined in your sales process. The individual "hunter" method of doing things their way, without any consideration to the larger corporate goals, can be very damaging to your sales organization in a broader sense. What these "lone wolf" individuals produce in revenue or GP in one area may actually be costing the company significant revenue or cost in other areas.

CUSTOMER AND PRODUCT APTITUDE

Many sales representatives can describe what something does. Or what features a certain product may have. Or they may even be able to recite the specific benefits of a product. The best salespeople are able to outline what this "means" to a customer, with an innate sense of conceptualizing the customer's experience and perspective. Many companies focus heavy-handedly on a sales representative's "industry experience" within a LOB when making hiring decisions. Assessing a sales representative's relational and cognitive ability to creatively solve problems for their customer will produce far greater top-line revenue growth in the longer term.

MINUS FACTORS OF VARIATION IN THE SALES PROCESS

Sales process issues are usually not dependent responsibilities for a salesperson in the hiring process because obviously the sales representative has never had the opportunity to operate in the confines of your process. But when discovering how a salesperson obtained previous results, it sometimes provides sharpened insight when clarity is given to understanding how the exploitation of someone else's sales process unduly contributed to a result.

So what does this all mean with respect to revenue generation? If explored properly, these four factors will often explain whether or not a salesperson will be the correct fit for your organization in their capacity to produce revenue growth for you. Investing in the right hiring process means you will have the right people in place from the onset to execute your sales strategy. Attaching rigor to the discipline of hiring exceptional sales staff, in alignment with your sales process, means the process can be executed upon with purpose and velocity.

Your salespeople, operating in conjunction with a consistent, stable and well-defined sales process is what drives outperformance in your revenue generation endeavors. However, because your sales managers know these factors of success far more intimately than an HR recruiter might, the key for making this hiring model work is that your sales managers should be "in the field", constantly seeking out new talent and informally assessing that talent, even when there are no open positions available in the organization.

Networking should be central to your sales management team's overall talent management master plan, perhaps even as a KPI expectation. And your HR staff should be enlisted, on-going, to be willing to hear the stories of potential new sales hires. That continual development of future bench strength makes it far easier to execute upon hiring exceptional talent when a need to hire suddenly arises. It is the difference between proactively preparing your success or simply reacting as circumstance dictates.

People animate process. It bears repeating. Effective hiring conventions are central to powerful sales management practice and are crucial for positioning your sales team for outstanding revenue growth.

VALUE 4: PUTTING THE CUSTOMER FIRST

By Richard Brune

A few years ago I worked with a client in the cherry processing business--one of three premier national suppliers. We'll call this company Premium Cherries. Premium Cherries had great market penetration with their Maraschino cherries, having sold their Maraschino cherries to nearly every QSR (Quick Serve Restaurant) in the marketplace. Premium's revenues were down and the economy was flat when I began working with Premium Cherries.

Premium Cherries had been successful in positioning their Maraschino's as a garnishment on top of milk shakes for a the largest QSR that was revamping its entire drink category, but the sales team was not proactive in closing the deal. When I began my engagement, the sales team was just waiting around for the QSR to call back with a signed purchase order. The first thing I did was set an appointment to visit the QSR's purchasing team and establish a relationship. Premium Cherries' VP of Sales, the National Account Manager and I were given 30 minutes to make our pitch so we put together a Power Point presentation on the virtues and our perceived key value proposition – our status as a farm to fork supplier.

When the time of the meeting arrived, I sensed that the VP of Sales and the National Account Manager wanted to jump right into the presentation after just a few minutes rapport building. Luckily, before they could do so, I jumped in. "Jane, we have done business with nearly every QSR in the United States. We've never sold yours and quite frankly do not want to assume anything. So I'm curious, what is important to you in a supplier?"

The scowling buyer had been sitting back in her chair, arms folded. She admitted the 30 minutes given to us was merely a courtesy since our two largest competitors had already been in her office and won the business. There was little to no chance we were going to take it away from the incumbents at this point, but after hearing my question, she unfolded her arms, leaned forward and said, "I'll tell you what's important to me - food safety, food quality, uninterrupted supply and price. The truth is, I'd pay more for the first three."

We walked into that meeting assuming that farm to fork was the most important thing to tell the buyer because it was our most important value proposition. Still wanting to dig deeper, I said, "Of those four, which is the most important to you?"

The buyer didn't hesitate. "Food safety is the corporate focus, food quality is expected, but what I really need is uninterrupted supply. When I walk into my office Monday morning, the last thing I need is to find out a restaurant ran out of cherries."

Now that we knew what was important to the buyer, we changed the entire pitch and focused on our ability to ensure on time deliveries consistently. If we had skipped asking a few questions at the beginning of our 30 minutes, we would certainly have walked away empty handed. But instead, our 30 minute meeting turned into 2 hours. The buyer began to see us as a trusted advisor instead of sales people who just want to close a deal. Because of this trust, we were able to uncover more needs that we could fulfill – such as helping them plot their expansion of this new version of a milk shake to all locations nationally. We served the customer for 5 months before ever getting a single purchase order. Because of the way we demonstrated a commitment to put them first with no obligation on their part, we ended up with 52% of their business the following year. And the best part, our price was the highest of the three suppliers – the other two splitting the remaining volume.

The lesson is simple, and one I'll never forget. Great companies and sales people don't see a customer as merely a person to sell to. Great companies and sales people see a customer as person with real needs, and after discovering what those needs are; put the customer first by serving and solving problems.

VALUE 5: SELL WITH STORY

By Justin Blaney

When I arrived at Umpqua Bank in downtown Bellevue, Washington I was ushered through a door that said Employees Only and down a short hall to a corner office. Inside, ten business leaders sat around a table laughing, handing out business cards and catching up. Since I was the last to arrive, we began shortly after I found my seat. For a half hour, we each described our work to the group, giving an elevator pitch for what makes us unique and the kinds of people we do business with. This group exists for cultivating a referral network and if you haven't been to a meeting like this, you may not realize how common it is. These meetings are happening in boardrooms, coffee shops and small town city halls around the country every day.

After the initial introductions were complete, a man in his mid-fifties named Will, who specializes in fractional CFO work, went into his spotlight presentation. Usually—if I can be honest with you— these presentations are pretty dry. Well-meaning presenters often break many of the ten commandments of public speaking such as cramming too many excel spreadsheets on a slide, reading from notes or saying um more often than I get passed on the freeway when my dad is driving. But this presentation was different. Will started by telling a story. He told us about his childhood, how his father owned and operated a dairy farm that made the best ice cream for a hundred miles. How his dad worked seven days a week, taking no more than an hour for dinner before returning to work each evening. Will didn't resent his father taking so much time for his business. He recognized, then and now, that running your own business can run you. Will's father didn't know there was any other way.

During this story, Will didn't use any slides or notes and he never once said um. He seemed at ease and confident, though I don't think it was because he'd practiced twenty times in front of the mirror that morning. I think it was because he was telling his own story. I looked around the room at one point and noticed that not a single person was checking their phone. Many were leaning forward. They interrupted Will with questions. They laughed at his jokes. And when Will said that his dream is to help leaders get into the driver's seat of their businesses rather than being run over by them, everyone believed him. This all happened a few days ago and I can't remember any of Will's other points. But I have a feeling I'm going to remember Will's story for a long time. I can picture him as a child, wishing his father was around to play ball. And I can feel Will's passion for helping today's business leaders avoid the fate of his father.

THE BEST SALESPEOPLE ARE REMEMBERED BY THEIR COLLEAGUES WHEN A NEED ARISES.

If someone asks you for a real estate agent, which one do you refer? You might find you actually know ten, but only one or two come to mind in the moment. Will did a fantastic job making himself memorable, and he's far more likely to come to my mind now when I hear about a business that might need his services. The same is true in many contexts of leadership, influence and life. If we become better storytellers, we're going to be more memorable, increase our influence and help more people grow.

THE ESSENCE OF STORY

Story is a powerful tool for communicating who you are, why people should care and how they can engage with you. It's important to understand the elements of story in light of helping you hone your own fairytale, where you're the hero.

I thought I was being original when I picked storytelling as the topic for one of my first breakout sessions at a marketing conference. I ran into one of the keynote speakers in the greenroom, an author well-known for his ability to take dry subjects and make them engaging through story. When he asked what my breakout topic was, I proudly gave my title.

"Your speaking about story?" he said. Something about the way he asked it took the shine off my hopes of impressing him.

I straightened my shoulders. "Yeah. I thought it would be cool to help marketers engage their audiences better through story."

As he turned to scan the room for someone more important he said, "Oh great, I wonder if anyone at this conference isn't speaking about story."

I grabbed a schedule and sure enough, most of the topics had something to do with storytelling. Titles like What story does your website tell? and Sell with story! and Your clothes tell a story, are they telling the right one? I began to realize that story had been hijacked.

People aren't marketers anymore. They're storytellers. Today, everything must tell a story. Even if there is no story to tell. Your website must tell a story. Same for your packaging, office's ingress, fleet and, of course, the clothes you wear. The problem is, culture seems to be forgetting that stories weren't invented yesterday. Story is an actual thing that has been around for a really long time, as long as humans have roamed the fruited plain. Now I admit, it sounds a lot cooler to sell a story rather than just a plain old boring website. And websites can in fact tell a story, but many people who sell storytelling websites, wardrobes or marketing plans are telling stories themselves, with much exaggeration, and they're confusing a lot of people in the process.

SO WHAT IS STORY ANYWAY?

In order to answer that question, we have to understand where story came from.

Stories were first told around fires. They were told by travelers, mothers, fathers, jesters, kings and fools. Uncles told stories about the elk that got away. Sisters tattled about brothers who pushed them in the river. Women told stories about how their husbands courted them. Men added details to those stories, noting how they'd loved their wives for two whole years before their wives would give them the time of day. Stories, at their most basic form, are a series of events. They're a plot. One could distill it down to a grocery list of events that are recounted in chronological order. But no mere series of events is going to be an engaging story in and of itself. Recounting my afternoon of meetings in painstaking detail isn't going to keep anyone's attention for more than about 10 seconds. Good stories, the ones worth telling, all have one thing in common: change.

In every story, someone changes. Sure circumstances change too, but it's the people in the stories we're most concerned with. Humans are social creatures and we want to hear about other people, even if those people are robots, animals or plants with human traits. Stories are about people changing. That's why stories were so important in the earlier years of our civilization, and why they remain important to this day. Stories are how we warn each other. They're how we raise our children. They're how we convince each other to do something, such as buying a stereo. They're how we inspire each other to stretch ourselves to reach our potential. This element is what's often missing from what people call stories. Too many think telling stories is simply recounting what happened, how they got here. But effective stories are centered on change. When you're selling something, what you're selling usually plays a central role in that change, i.e. your client's business was falling apart until they hired your consulting firm and now everything has changed for them.

STORIES ARE INFINITELY MORE EASY TO REMEMBER THAN FACTOIDS.

Just think back to history class. Do you remember all the critical dates of the Civil War? Not likely. But I bet you remember the stories. You might even be able to picture movies you've seen about the war or recall the books you've read. You think about the people, even if you can't remember their names. You think about what was at stake and the lives that were changed. Most companies sell facts and features. Great companies sell stories. Great companies also use elements of story to improve their connection to customers. For example, most clothing companies show ads of beautiful people in beautiful locations with other beautiful people having fun or just looking cool. This is a form of scene setting and they're inviting the audience or target market to insert themselves into the scene. It's a sort of interactive storytelling element that allows the audience to enter into the story. And it only costs $119 for the dress that will take you there. This isn't a story, but it's an element of a story. And it allows you to imagine the life transformation you'll experience by purchasing the clothes and entering into the story the company is telling.

You can use this kind of lifestyle scene setting to your benefit, but it tends to be the method used by big budget advertisers. A more cost effective use of storytelling is simply recounting how a customer engaged with you and how their business was transformed. The beauty of this kind of storytelling is you don't even need to advertise your company. In fact, you should diminish your role as much as possible. Make the star of the story your customer. Your target market will connect the dots on their own and realize that you played an important role in that transformation.

GOOD STORIES ARE EASY TO REMEMBER AND SHARE.

When they feature what you do, how you do it and how a client is able to purchase it, it makes it easier for your target market to remember what you do and how they can access it for themselves. Keep telling these stories over and over every chance you get and over time people will actually start to remember what you said. It still takes awhile, but it will happen a lot faster than if you just spam people with boring facts about your company. The attraction to selling stories instead of whatever else people are hawking these days is that great storytelling has always been and will always be in demand. There is no technology, no industry change, no outsourcing opportunity, no economic downturn that will replace or reduce the need for story. The business model, the distribution system, the method of payment may change a million times, but a great storyteller will always have a place at the fire.

This chapter is an excerpt from the book Famously Helpful. You can download a complete copy at www.famouslyhelpful.com or purchase a paperback copy on Amazon.

VALUE 6: LESS IS MORE

By Dean Kato

We have all suffered through presentations where a salesperson expands ten minutes of worthwhile content into an hour of our time. It's hard to follow, not always what you need to know and you're left with unanswered questions. How does a presenter avoid these pitfalls? Over time, I've learned three philosophies that help create more focused and effective sales presentations.

KNOW YOUR AUDIENCE

I once went into a meeting with a prospective customer and gave my standard presentation, discussing our technical features and discriminators. About half way through, one person in the audience said "This is all good stuff, but we're all buyers and are just looking for cost reduction solutions – this presentation would be better for our engineers." Oops.

We all have a "canned" presentation – twenty-five slides intended to take an hour that we have memorized and are very comfortable with. Although this may be the easiest presentation for us to give, it may not be the most effective to our potential customer. Key to making your interaction resonate is to know what is important to the recipient; emphasize what problem you can solve (i.e cost reduction) and not what you have to sell.

Knowing to whom you're presenting, and what is important to them, needs preparation and homework.

- Are they executives, managers or individual contributors?
- Have they historically utilized your type of service or product?
- Do they work with a competitor?
- Do you have an internal "coach" who can guide you on what is important?

Start with as much information as possible about which characteristics are important.

- Is speed of fulfillment more important than price?

- Ordering simplicity and online presence a key?
- Competitive pricing?
- Subject matter expertise?

NOTHING MARGINALIZES YOUR PRESENTATION MORE THAN MISSING THE MARK ON WHAT IS OF INTEREST TO YOUR AUDIENCE

What is the culture and expectation for presentations? It's easy to assume you have an hour and a half to present, and a visual PowerPoint® is expected, but keep these questions in mind.

- What is the culture and expectation for presentations?
- Are they expecting a fifteen-minute standup meeting?
- Bulleted list of topics, or full artwork and graphics?
- Are there any items in your presentation that could require sensitivity to compliance or export? Such as government work.
- Is there a company dress code?

Once you know whom you are presenting to, make sure your material is succinct and focused.

LESS IS MORE

Don't let your audience tune out and start counting the seconds until the end of the meeting! If we've done a good job of knowing our audience, we should have a good handle on what is important and how to target specific issues rather than droning on about every possible related specification, variation, or color of product available.

Years ago, many meetings were an hour long by default. More recently, business culture has changed to 30 or 15 minute meetings as the norm. Some organizations even have "standup" meetings to keep people focused on just the topic at hand. It's more essential to present only what's important to the audience. So what can you do to ensure an effective presentation?

Start with a very short overview, and be prepared to focus and elaborate on specific areas of interest. Have a deck of backup slides that allow you to go deeper if your audience asks for that. If your prospect says "Sounds good, let's do it" half way through your presentation, you are done! Don't oversell because you didn't get to finish your presentation.

Slides should have a limited amount of large, legible text in outline form. Jokes about "this is an eye chart" may seem funny, but do nothing to help your presentation. Don't read directly off the slide. Your knowledge should be sufficient to elaborate on the outlined material on each slide, emphasizing what you know to be of interest.

Always leave them wanting more; a valid business reason to follow up with additional information!

I always feel good about a short meeting that ends with "You hit all our areas of interest."

PRACTICE A HIGH LISTEN TO TALK RATIO

As salespeople, we enjoy making presentations and hearing ourselves talk. Why not, we have very important information to impart! This is often to the detriment of our goal which is to create more interest in our presentation material and to close a sale.

Nothing makes you a better presenter or conversationalist than finding more information about your audience. Genuine interest in their needs will strike an important chord. It's easy to believe we are experts in our topic, and if we ask questions we would only exhibit uncertainty or a lack of knowledge. The opposite in fact is true. Targeted questions allow us to zero in on the exact issues that are of importance to our audience.

Active listening is possibly more important than the material I prepared. This helps you in understanding:

- Am I on target addressing issues important to you?
- What are your "pain points" I am able to address?
- How can I really serve you?

A skilled presenter can make adjustments on the fly. Real-time feedback from the audience can help us shape the presentation as we go along.

One presentation I started with a group of engineers was focused on solutions we were proposing to a problem at hand. After the first ten minutes, it became evident the real problem statement had little to do with our products, the issues were at a more basic level. I closed the presentation and sat down at the table. For the balance of the time we had an effective brainstorming session. This served to increase my credibility with the customer. At that point, I wasn't selling, I was part of the solution.

These concepts are universal when interacting with people. Whether one on one or in large groups. Practice these three easy rules and you will significantly increase the effectiveness of your presentations.

VALUE 7: GREAT ONE-ON-ONES

By Glenn Hansen

When I ask sales managers, what is the single most effective thing they can do to grow sales revenue, they usually struggle with their answer.

After a brief discussion, they always agree: the most effective thing they can do is to manage each of their sales people in such a way their individual sales performance brings greater sales growth.

To do this most effectively, sales managers must have regularly scheduled, one-on-one, performance management meetings. The timing is usually one per week. If their sales people are traveling and the meetings can't be done in person, it is still important to have the meeting by Skype or phone.

Start by setting very clear expectations about when the weekly meetings will take place, how long they will be and what the sales person is expected to bring to the meeting. These expectations should be in writing.

For example: Let's say a weekly one-on-one is at 8:00am every Monday morning. The meeting will last no more than 30 minutes. Some weeks it may only last 15 or 20 minutes.

THINGS TO REVIEW IN THE ONE-ON-ONE

Each week have a written plan for what sales-generating activities they intend to perform in the upcoming week. Review what they actually did, compare it to their plan from the previous week. Then, review their plan for the upcoming week. Coach, encourage, challenge and affirm.

TYPES OF ACTIVITIES

- Cold calls
- Warm calls
- Follow-up calls
- Relationship nurturing calls

- Onsite calls
- Presentations
- Proposals

SALES PIPELINE FOR REVIEW AND COACHING

Have sales person explain where they are with their various prospects and what they have done in the last week to move them through the pipeline.

SKILLS DEVELOPMENT

Each sales person should be learning and developing something each week to improve their effectiveness and subsequently, their close rate. They might be working on product knowledge, sales skills, or some other personal development.

Example: Perhaps they are on a quest to ask more effective questions. The sales manager will ask what they have learned in the last week then provide some coaching, perhaps role-playing.

Weekly one-on-one performance management meetings will become more effective over time. To ensure the sales manager brings out the best in sales people and see their sales grow, follow these five steps in executing the weekly meetings:

1. Set clear expectations

2. Teach and coach

3. Review what you expect

4. Affirm good efforts, execution and performance

5. Hold them accountable for what you expect.

I have taught this to many sales managers over the years and they have been amazed at how impactful THEY could be in driving up sales through their weekly one-on-one's.

"Mike" is an example. He had been a sales manager for five years. He'd worked hard and seen sales in his department grow. After he had been doing weekly one-on-ones for several months, he saw the impressive results he was achieving. He declared to me one day with humility, "You know, Glenn, I am REALLY good at this!" If a sales manager is a leader, their sales people respect him/her and want to perform well, AND the Sales Manager executes effective weekly one-on-one performance management meetings, you may be amazed at how much you will see sales grow!

ABOUT ONEACCORD

OneAccord works with mid-market companies and organizations, both for-profit and nonprofit, to change the trajectory of revenue growth.

OUR PRINCIPALS UNDERSTAND HOW TO RUN A BUSINESS.

They aren't "consultants," but operators with substantial top-line revenue experience. They aren't trying to climb any corporate ladder, are comfortable with what they know, and don't know, and tell the truth.

EVERY ENGAGEMENT IS DIFFERENT.

OneAccord begins engagements with our Revenue Review.

Unlike a traditional "consulting firm" looking to provide reports, we will either validate your existing plan or point to clear revenue opportunities in rapid fashion. Given that our team is comprised of operating executives, the turn-around is in a fraction of the time.

The Revenue Review also provides an accurate baseline for customizing a revenue plan for your company.

When you need to change the trajectory of your organization's growth and achieve new levels of effectiveness, contact OneAccord; our Principals are ready to help.

FIND OUT MORE AT
WWW.ONEACCORDPARTNERS.COM

ABOUT THE AUTHORS

JUSTIN BLANEY

Justin R. Blaney D.M. is the managing partner of click.works, a OneAccord company. He is also a speaker, entrepreneur and #1 bestselling author of 14 books who has helped thousands of individuals and organizations increase influence and generate demand for their ideas, products, and services. Justin and his family live outside Seattle.

RICHARD BRUNE

Richard Brune is a sales and marketing professional with over 25 years of experience in building and managing some of America's most recognizable consumer brands.

Richard has an unbroken record of substantial sales and market share increases with such brands as Stanley Tools, Hartmann Luggage, REI Inc., Swiss Army Brands and licensed products with Eddie Bauer and Disney.

GLENN HANSEN

For 25 years, Glenn was a highly success retail management senior executive in the consumer electronics industry. Achieving extraordinary results and leading profitable sales and retail stores, he builds teams with synergy. He has lead teams to success in vastly different sales environments for both products and services.

He is a great sales trainer and motivator. Glenn also has a talent for building effective strategies amidst complex challenges and takes strategy to execution to achieve and exceed goals. In all, Glenn is a 'best in class' result-getter.

JOHN KAMINSKI

John Kaminski has over 25 years experience in sales and marketing. He began his sales career with Xerox and went on to work in the medical device industry prior to starting his own business. John has been recognized as a top performer at every company with which he has worked.

John excels at business-to-business sales and marketing strategy, including bringing structure to the sales process, and selling into the executive suite. He is passionate about helping businesses establish a winning culture and growing exponentially.

DEAN KATO

For over 30 years, Dean Kato has created growth and customer relationships for organizations both large and small. His customer base has included such organizations as Boeing, EMBRAER, Airbus, Longs Drugs, non-profits, and the US Government. His focus throughout has been creating win-win opportunities by doing the right thing and serving rather than selling. His current clients look to Dean for guidance in optimizing manufacturing operations and top line growth

JEFF ROGERS

Originally from Edmonds, WA, Jeff graduated from the University of Washington with a degree in Finance and Marketing. He has been involved in both sales and management development for over 25 years and is Founder of OneAccord. Jeff is involved in coaching basketball and soccer, enjoys skiing and fishing, and is founder and President of Kiros.